TAYLOR SWIFT

KATIE LAJINESS

Big Buddy Books

An Imprint of Abdo Publishing
abdopublishing.com

BIG Buddy POP BIOGRAPHIES

abdopublishing.com

Published by Abdo Publishing, a division of ABDO, PO Box 398166, Minneapolis, Minnesota 55439.
Copyright © 2016 by Abdo Consulting Group, Inc. International copyrights reserved in all countries.
No part of this book may be reproduced in any form without written permission from the publisher.
Big Buddy Books™ is a trademark and logo of Abdo Publishing.

Printed in the United States of America, North Mankato, Minnesota.
102015
012016

THIS BOOK CONTAINS
RECYCLED MATERIALS

Cover Photo: Dan MacMedan/ Getty Images.
Interior Photos: Associated Press (pp. 9, 15, 17, 27); Charley Gallay/Getty Images (p. 6); Scott
    Gries/Getty Images (p. 13); © iStockphoto.com (p. 11); Eric Jamison/Invision/AP (p. 29);
    © Andrew Orth/Retna Ltd/Corbis (p. 9); Christopher Polk/MTV1415/Getty Images (p. 21); John
    Salangsang/Invision/AP (p. 5); Matt Sayles/Invision/AP (pp. 23, 31); John Shearer/Invision/AP
    (p. 19); Charles Sykes/Invision/AP (p. 25); Amy T. Zielinski/Getty Images (p. 19).

Coordinating Series Editor: Tamara L. Britton
Contributing Editor: Marcia Zappa
Graphic Design: Jenny Christensen

Library of Congress Cataloging-in-Publication Data

Lajiness, Katie, author.
  Taylor Swift / Katie Lajiness.
      pages cm. -- (Big buddy pop biographies)
  Includes index.
  ISBN 978-1-68078-060-4
1. Swift, Taylor, 1989---Juvenile literature. 2. Country musicians--United States--Biography--Juvenile
literature. I. Title.
  ML3930.S989L35 2016
  782.421642092--dc23
  [B]
                              2015033047

CONTENTS

MUSIC SENSATION 4

SNAPSHOT 5

FAMILY TIES 6

EARLY YEARS................................... 8

RISING STAR 10

BUILDING A CAREER 14

POP PRINCESS................................18

AWARD SHOWS 22

GIVING BACK 24

ACTING CAREER 26

BUZZ...28

GLOSSARY....................................30

WEBSITES....................................31

INDEX 32

MUSIC SENSATION

Taylor Swift is a talented singer and songwriter. She is known for her country and **pop** music. Taylor has won **awards** for her hit albums and songs.

With many hit songs, Taylor's music has made her famous. She has appeared on magazine covers. Taylor has also been **interviewed** on popular television shows.

SNAPSHOT

NAME:
Taylor Alison Swift

BIRTHDAY:
December 13, 1989

BIRTHPLACE:
Reading, Pennsylvania

POPULAR ALBUMS:
Speak Now, Red, 1989

FAMILY TIES

Taylor Alison Swift was born in Reading, Pennsylvania, on December 13, 1989. Her parents are Scott and Andrea Swift. Taylor has a younger brother named Austin.

Taylor often attended events with her family. In 2014, she and her brother, Austin Swift, went to a party after the Golden Globe Awards.

WHERE IN THE WORLD?

CANADA

New York

Pennsylvania

Ohio

Reading

New Jersey

ATLANTIC
OCEAN

West Virginia

Maryland

Virginia

Delaware

N

W E

S

EARLY YEARS

As a child, Taylor loved music! She started singing at age five. When she was ten years old, Taylor began to sing at public events such as fairs. Two years later, she learned to play the **guitar**.

DID YOU KNOW ?

Taylor grew up on a Christmas tree farm! During the holidays, she helped sell Christmas trees from the farm.

Taylor wrote her first song in the third grade! She named it "Your Song."

Taylor plays chords on her guitar. A chord is a group of tones sounded together to form harmony.

RISING STAR

When she was 14, Taylor and her family moved to the Nashville, Tennessee area. There, she continued to write songs. But, Taylor wanted to sing, too.

In 2005, Taylor signed a contract with Big Machine Records. She wrote or helped write all of the songs on her first album!

Nashville is known for country music. Many people there work in the music business.

In summer 2006, Taylor **released** her first single, "Tim McGraw." The song was a hit! In October, *Taylor Swift* **debuted**. This album produced popular singles such as "Our Song," "Picture to Burn," "Should've Said No," and "Teardrops on My **Guitar**."

In 2007, Taylor sang "Our Song" at the Country Music Association Awards.

BUILDING A CAREER

Fans were excited to hear which songs Taylor would sing on her second album. In September 2008, "Love Story" **debuted** as the first official single. It sold more than 5 million copies!

In November 2008, *Fearless* was **released**. It was number one on the Billboard 200 album chart. With two best-selling records, Taylor was a superstar!

In 2009, Taylor won the Academy of Country Music's Album of the Year for *Fearless*!

In 2010, Taylor **released** her third studio album, *Speak Now*. She wrote every song on the album!

Two years later, Taylor released *Red*. This record sold more than 1.2 million copies in its first week. This means two albums were sold every second!

DID YOU KNOW?

Speak Now produced 11 hit singles! Taylor was the first artist to have that many hit singles on one album.

In 2011, Taylor went on a world tour to support *Speak Now*. She performed in 18 different countries.

POP PRINCESS

In 2014, Taylor **released** her first fully **pop**-music album, *1989*. It was the top-selling album of 2014. It sold more than 3.6 million copies in nine weeks!

DID YOU KNOW?
Taylor spent two years writing songs for *1989*!

For Taylor's *1989* album, she worked with singers Imogen Heap (*left*) and Ryan Tedder (*below*).

That same year, Taylor moved to New York City, New York. Her move fit nicely with a song on *1989* called "Welcome to New York."

The album also included hit songs such as "Bad Blood," "Blank Space," and "Shake It Off." In July 2015, Taylor's music video for "Blank Space" had more than 1 billion views on the **social media** site YouTube!

Taylor won Video of the Year at the 2015 MTV Video Music Awards for her "Bad Blood" music video.

AWARD SHOWS

As a popular singer, Taylor is no stranger to **award** shows. There, she often **performs** her latest song. In 2014, Taylor played the piano and sang "All Too Well" at the **Grammy Awards**.

Taylor has won many awards for her music. As of 2015, she has accepted seven Grammy Awards. With her 20 Billboard Music Awards, Taylor is the most decorated artist in the show's history!

In November 2014, Taylor won the Dick Clark Award for Excellence at the American Music Awards. This was the first time anyone had won this award.

GIVING BACK

Taylor loves to help out kids! In 2012, she gave 14,000 children's books to Nashville public libraries. And, in 2014 Taylor visited a New York City children's hospital. She spent time with sick kids.

As her fans know, Taylor is a very giving person. In 2015, she promised to give money earned from her song "Welcome to New York" to the city's public schools.

In 2014, Taylor attended a benefit for the Metropolitan Museum of Art in New York City.

ACTING CAREER

Taylor is also an actress! She has appeared in movies and television shows.

In 2012, Taylor was a voice actor in *The Lorax*. This is a movie based on the Dr. Seuss book. She was the voice of Audrey.

In 2014, Taylor had a **role** in *The Giver*. In this movie, she wore a brown wig to hide her **pop**-star look.

DID YOU KNOW
In 2013, Taylor was on the television show *New Girl*.

Taylor attended the world premiere of *The Lorax* in Los Angeles, California.

BUZZ

In 2015, Taylor had a very busy year! She won Song of the Year for "Shake It Off" at the iHeartRadio Music **Awards**.

From May 2015 to October 2015, Taylor was on the road for her 1989 World Tour. She traveled to five countries.

Taylor is such a talented artist. Her music keeps getting bigger and better. Fans are excited to see what Taylor does next!

In 2015, Taylor won eight Billboard Music Awards! She won the Top Artist and Top Female Artist awards, among others.

GLOSSARY

award something that is given in recognition of good work or a good act.

debut (DAY-byoo) to make a first appearance.

Grammy Award any of the awards given each year by the National Academy of Recording Arts and Sciences. Grammy Awards honor the year's best accomplishments in music.

guitar (guh-TAHR) a stringed musical instrument played by strumming.

interview to ask someone a series of questions.

perform to do something in front of an audience.

pop relating to popular music.

release to make available to the public.

role a part an actor plays.

social media a form of communication on the Internet where people can share information, messages, and videos. It may include blogs and online groups.

WEBSITES

To learn more about Pop Biographies, visit **booklinks.abdopublishing.com**.
These links are routinely monitored and updated to provide
the most current information available.

INDEX

awards **4, 6, 13, 14, 15, 21, 22, 23, 28, 29**

Big Machine Records **10**

California **27**

charity work **24, 25**

Fearless (album) **14, 15**

Giver, The (movie) **26**

Heap, Imogen **19**

Lorax, The (movie) **26, 27**

McGraw, Tim **12**

New Girl (television show) **26**

New York **20, 24, 25**

1989 (album) **5, 18, 19, 20**

1989 World Tour **28**

Pennsylvania **5, 6**

Rascall Flatts **12**

Red (album) **5, 16**

Speak Now (album) **5, 16, 17**

Speak Now World Tour **17**

Swift, Andrea **6**

Swift, Austin **6**

Swift, Scott **6**

Taylor Swift (album) **10, 12**

Tedder, Ryan **19**

Tennessee **10, 11, 24**